LOVE
&
THE MERRY-GO-ROUND

Poems chosen by
Rosemary Harris

illustrated by
Pauline Baynes

Hamish Hamilton · London

For Barbara, my mother, with love

HAMISH HAMILTON CHILDREN'S BOOKS

Published by the Penguin Group
27 Wrights Lane, London W8 5TZ, England
Viking Penguin Inc., 40 West 23rd Street, New York, New York 10010, USA
Penguin Books Australia Ltd, Ringwood, Victoria, Australia
Penguin Books Canada Ltd, 2801 John Street, Markham, Ontario, Canada L3R 1B4
Penguin Books (NZ) Ltd, 182–190 Wairau Road, Auckland 10, New Zealand

Penguin Books Ltd, Registered Offices: Harmondsworth, Middlesex, England

First published in Great Britain 1988 by
Hamish Hamilton Children's Books

This selection copyright © 1988 by Rosemary Harris
Illustrations copyright © 1988 by Pauline Baynes
Copyright information for individual poems is given on page 89
which constitute an extension of this copyright page.

All rights reserved. Without limiting the rights under copyright reserved above, no part of this publication may be reproduced, stored in or introduced into a retrieval system or transmitted, in any form or by any means (electronic, mechanical, photocopying, recording or otherwise), without the prior written permission of both the copyright owner and the above publisher of this book.

British Library Cataloguing in Publication Data
Harris, Rosemary
Love & the merry-go-round.
I. Title
821'.914   PZ83

ISBN 0-241-12412-3

Typeset by CentraCet
Printed and bound in Great Britain by
Butler & Tanner Ltd, Frome, Somerset

Contents

Foreword	Rosemary Harris	5
Morning Song	Sylvia Plath	7
Adam	Rainer Maria Rilke	8
Eve	Rainer Maria Rilke	9
A Dream of Nourishment	Stevie Smith	10
Fern Hill	Dylan Thomas	11
Allie	Robert Graves	14
True Sympathy	G. K. Chesterton	16
The Heart's Journey IV	Siegfried Sassoon	18
Song: Dew-Drop and Diamond	Robert Graves	19
The Merry-go-round	Rainer Maria Rilke	20
Fancy's Knell	A. E. Housman	22
Molly Gone	Thomas Hardy	24
Fafaïa	Rupert Brooke	26
A Weather Spell	Elizabeth Jennings	27
Song	Ted Hughes	28
A Last Confession	W. B. Yeats	29
To Women, as Far As I'm Concerned	D. H. Lawrence	30
The People Upstairs	Ogden Nash	31
You on the Tower	Thomas Hardy	32
Friendship	Elizabeth Jennings	34
Move On	William Plomer	35
Hawthorn White	Charles Causley	36
My Hat	Stevie Smith	38
Sent from the Capital to her Elder Daughter	Lady Ōtomo of Sakanoue	39
Lyrics from the Chinese: v	Helen Waddell	40
Hamra Night	Sa'di Yusuf	41
Winter Night	Boris Pasternak	42

I Like For You To Be Still	Pablo Neruda	44
The Skunk	Seamus Heaney	45
To Be Called a Bear	Robert Graves	46
The Licorice Fields at Pontefract	John Betjeman	47
Last Poems XXI	A. E. Housman	48
Last Poems XXIII	A. E. Housman	49
The Hill	Rupert Brooke	50
Love Poem	Elizabeth Jennings	51
For Ann Scott-Moncrieff (1914–1943)	Edwin Muir	52
In Love for Long	Edwin Muir	54
All That's Past	Walter de la Mare	56
Here Lies a Lady	John Crowe Ransom	57
9th Century Requiem	Helen Waddell	58
Boy in Ice	Laurie Lee	59
Alexander	Walter de la Mare	60
Cities and Thrones and Powers	Rudyard Kipling	62
Mortality	John Betjeman	63
Miss Robinson's Funeral	William Plomer	64
my sweet old etcetera	e. e. cummings	65
Grizabella: the Glamour Cat	T. S. Eliot	66
Memory	Trevor Nunn	67
In Valleys Green and Still	A. E. Housman	69
Miners	Wilfred Owen	70
Be Not Amazed	Léopold Sédar Senghor	72
In the Pink	Siegfried Sassoon	73
At the Cenotaph	Siegfried Sassoon	74
Fire and Ice	Robert Frost	75
The Horses of Achilles	C. P. Cavafy	76
My Heart Goes Out	Stevie Smith	77
One Flesh	Elizabeth Jennings	78
Girl's Song	W. B. Yeats	79
An Old Man	C. P. Cavafy	80
Grandfather's Holiday	Rabindranath Tagore	81
The Song of Wandering Aengus	W. B. Yeats	82
If I Could Tell You	W. H. Auden	83
The Airy Christ	Stevie Smith	84
The Conversation of Prayer	Dylan Thomas	85
The Arrival of the Bee Box	Sylvia Plath	86
I Am the Great Sun	Charles Causley	88

FOREWORD

IT ALMOST seems that a selection of poetry, however short, should begin with apologies for what has been left out – although to make a choice among great riches is almost impossible, and grows harder still when wading through the treasure-house of poems that span the last hundred years. Anyway, this is only a little book, limited in space, which has been put together for enjoyment's sake; and more in the hope of giving pleasure to a new readership and encouraging it to look further, than in attempting to cover too wide a field. Only thirty-eight poets are represented, and their poems deal largely with relating – to people, to love, war, death, and renewal.

When I was a child we were taken annually to a great fair at Ranelagh, where there was a huge, brilliantly-painted and entirely thrilling roundabout, and a smaller, gentler one for smaller people. But both went to the same type of tune, and on both the horses, cars and ostriches went quickly, and rose and fell, and slowed, and stopped. Some passengers got off, others stayed, joined by fresh riders. Some were laughing, occasionally there were tears. Then the whole show began revolving again; just like the symbolism in Rainer Maria Rilke's marvellous poem, 'The Merry-go-round', with its slightly ominous refrain.

Ominous, yes. Poets, I think, are quite dangerous people. For good or ill they wake us up, demanding that we try to see better, and understand. They are obsessed with what lies beneath appearance – with the challenges of love and time, and more uncomfortably and constantly aware than we are of the merry-go-round we ride and from which we all eventually dismount. Yet good poetry is fortifying, too. It deals with experience that will return like the spring; if not for us, then for someone else. Even after war and death comes a possibility of resurrection. The music starts up. Once more, as in Sylvia Plath's poem 'The Arrival of the Bee Box', the bees fly out to taste the spring.

Sylvia Plath

Morning Song

Love set you going like a fat gold watch.
The midwife slapped your footsoles, and your bald cry
Took its place among the elements.

Our voices echo, magnifying your arrival. New statue.
In a drafty museum, your nakedness
Shadows our safety. We stand round blankly as walls.

I'm no more your mother
Than the cloud that distills a mirror to reflect its own slow
Effacement at the wind's hand.

All night your moth-breath
Flickers among the flat pink roses. I wake to listen:
A far sea moves in my ear.

One cry, and I stumble from bed, cow-heavy and floral
In my Victorian nightgown.
Your mouth opens clean as a cat's. The window square

Whitens and swallows its dull stars. And now you try
Your handful of notes;
The clear vowels rise like balloons.

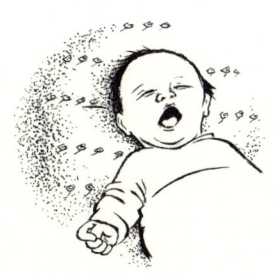

Rainer Maria Rilke

Adam

He, on the cathedral's steep ascent,
stands and stares near where the window-rose is,
as if awed by the apotheosis
which, when it had reached its full extent,

set him over these and these below.
And he towers and joys in his duration,
plain-resolved; who started cultivation
first of all mankind, and did not know

how he'd find a way from Eden-garden,
ready-filled with all it could supply,
to the new earth. God would only harden,

and, instead of granting him his prayer,
kept on threatening he should surely die.
But the man persisted: She will bear.

Rainer Maria Rilke

Eve

She, on the cathedral's vast ascent,
simply stands there near the window-rose,
with the apple in the apple-pose,
ever henceforth guilty – innocent

of the growingness she brought to birth
since that time she lovingly departed
from the old eternities and started
struggling like a young year through the earth.

Ah, she could have stayed so gladly, though,
just a little longer there, attending
to the sense and concord beasts would show.

But she found the man resolved to go,
so she went out with him, deathwards tending;
and yet God she'd scarcely got to know.

Stevie Smith

A Dream of Nourishment

I had a dream of nourishment
Against a breast
My infant face was presst
Ah me the *suffisance* I drew therefrom
What strength, what glory from that fattening fluid,
The fattening most
Was to my infant taste
For oh the sun of strength beat in my veins
And swelled me full, I lay in brightest sun
All ready to put forth, all bursting, all delight.

But in my dream the breast withdrew
In darkness I lay then
And thin,
Thin as a sheeted ghost
And I was famished,
Hankered for a dish
I thought, of blood, as in some classicist's
Old tale
To give me hue and substance, make me hale.

Oh breast, oh Best
That I held fast
Oh fattening draught
Timely repast
Quaffed, presst
And lost.

The breast was withdrawn violently
And oh the famishment for me.

Dylan Thomas

Fern Hill

Now as I was young and easy under the apple boughs
About the lilting house and happy as the grass was green,
    The night above the dingle starry,
        Time let me hail and climb
    Golden in the heydays of his eyes,
And honoured among wagons I was prince of the apple towns
And once below a time I lordly had the trees and leaves
        Trail with daisies and barley
    Down the rivers of the windfall light.

And as I was green and carefree, famous among the barns
About the happy yard and singing as the farm was home,
    In the sun that is young once only,
        Time let me play and be
    Golden in the mercy of his means,
And green and golden I was huntsman and herdsman, the
                                        calves
  Sang to my horn, the foxes on the hills barked clear and cold,
        And the sabbath rang slowly
    In the pebbles of the holy streams.

All the sun long it was running, it was lovely, the hay
Fields high as the house, the tunes from the chimneys, it was
                                            air

      And playing, lovely and watery
          And fire green as grass.
      And nightly under the simple stars
As I rode to sleep the owls were bearing the farm away,
All the moon long I heard, blessed among stables, the night-
                                            jars
      Flying with the ricks, and the horses
      Flashing into the dark.

And then to awake, and the farm, like a wanderer white
With the dew, come back, the cock on his shoulder: it was all
      Shining, it was Adam and maiden,
          The sky gathered again
          And the sun grew round that very day.
So it must have been after the birth of the simple light
In the first, spinning place, the spellbound horses walking
                                          warm
      Out of the whinnying green stable
      On to the fields of praise.

And honoured among foxes and pleasants by the gay house
Under the new made clouds and happy as the heart was long,
      In the sun born over and over,
          I ran my heedless ways,
      My wishes raced through the house high hay
And nothing I cared, at my sky blue trades, that time allows
In all his tuneful turning so few and such morning songs
      Before the children green and golden
          Follow him out of grace,

Nothing I cared, in the lamb white days, that time would take
$$\text{me}$$
Up to the swallow thronged loft by the shadow of my hand,
    In the moon that is always rising,
        Nor that riding to sleep
    I should hear him fly with the high fields
And wake to the farm forever fled from the childless land.
Oh as I was young and easy in the mercy of his means,
        Time held me green and dying
        Though I sang in my chains like the sea.

Robert Graves

Allie

Allie, call the birds in,
    The birds from the sky!
Allie calls, Allie sings,
    Down they all fly:
First there came
Two white doves,
    Then a sparrow from his nest,
Then a clucking bantam hen,
    Then a robin red-breast.

Allie, call the beasts in,
    The beasts, every one!
Allie calls, Allie sings,
    In they all run:
First there came
Two black lambs,
    Then a grunting Berkshire sow,
Then a dog without a tail,
    Then a red and white cow.

Allie, call the fish up,
    The fish from the stream!
Allie calls, Allie sings,
    Up they all swim:
First there came
Two gold fish,
    A minnow and a miller's thumb,
Then a school of little trout,
    Then the twisting eels come.

Allie, call the children,
    Call them from the green!
Allie calls, Allie sings,
    Soon they run in:
First there came
Tom and Madge,
    Kate and I who'll not forget
How we played by the water's edge
    Till the April sun set.

G. K. Chesterton

True Sympathy
or Prevention of Cruelty to Teachers

I was kind to all my masters
    And I never worked them hard
To goad them to exactitude
    Or speaking by the card.

If one of them should have the air
    Of talking through his hat
And call a curve isosceles
    I let it go at that.

The point was without magnitude;
    I knew without regret
Our minds were moving parallel
    Because they never met.

Because I could not bear to make
    An Algebraist cry
I gazed with interest at X
    And never thought of Why.

That he should think I thought he thought
    That X was ABC
Was far, far happier for him
    And possibly for me.

While other teachers raved and died
   In reason's wild career,
Men who had driven themselves mad
   By making themselves clear,

My teachers laugh and sing and dance,
   Aged, but still alive;
Because I often let them say
   That two and two are five.

Angles obtuse appeared acute,
   Angles acute were quite
Obtuse; but I was more obtuse;
   Their angles were all right.

I wore my Soul's Awakening smile,
   I felt it was my duty:
Lo! Logic works by Barbara
   And life is ruled by Beauty.

And Mathematics merged and met
   Its Higher Unity,
Where Five and Two and Twelve and Four
   They all were One to me.

Siegfried Sassoon

The Heart's Journey IV

What you are I cannot say;
Only this I know full well –
When I touched your face to-day
Drifts of blossom flushed and fell.

Whence you came I cannot tell;
Only – with your joy you start
Chime on chime from bell on bell
In the cloisters of my heart.

Robert Graves

Song: Dew-Drop and Diamond

The difference between you and her
(Whom I to you did once prefer)
Is clear enough to settle:
She like a diamond shone, but you
Shine like an early drop of dew
Poised on a red rose-petal.

The dew-drop carries in its eye
Mountain and forest, sea and sky,
With every change of weather;
Contrariwise, a diamond splits
The prospect into idle bits
That none can piece together.

Rainer Maria Rilke

The Merry-go-round
Jardin du Luxembourg

With roof and shadow for a while careers
the stud of horses, variously bright,
all from that land that long remains in sight
before it ultimately disappears.
Several indeed pull carriages, with tight-
held rein, but all have boldness in their bearing;
with them a wicked scarlet lion's faring
and now and then an elephant all white.

Just as in woods, a stag comes into view,
save that it has a saddle and tied fast
thereon a little maiden all in blue.

And on the lion a little boy is going,
whose small hot hands hold on with all his might,
while raging lion's tongue and teeth are showing.

And now and then an elephant all white.

And on the horses they come riding past,
girls too, bright-skirted, whom the horse-jumps here
scarce now preoccupy: in full career
elsewhither, hitherwards, a glance they cast –

And now and then an elephant all white.

And this keeps passing by until it's ended,
and hastens aimlessly until it's done.
A red, a green, a grey is apprehended,
a little profile, scarcely yet begun. –
And now and then a smile, for us intended,
blissfully happy, dazzlingly expended
upon this breathless, blindly followed fun . . .

A. E. Housman

Fancy's Knell

When lads were home from labour
    At Abdon under Clee,
A man would call his neighbour
    And both would send for me.
And where the light in lances
    Across the mead was laid,
There to the dances
    I fetched my flute and played.

Ours were idle pleasures,
    Yet oh, content we were,
The young to wind the measures,
    The old to heed the air;
And I to lift with playing
    From tree and tower and steep
The light delaying,
    And flute the sun to sleep.

The youth toward his fancy
    Would turn his brow of tan,
And Tom would pair with Nancy
    And Dick step off with Fan;
The girl would lift her glances
    To his, and both be mute:
Well went the dances
    At evening to the flute.

Wenlock Edge was umbered,
    And bright was Abdon Burf,
And warm between them slumbered
    The smooth green miles of turf;
Until from grass and clover
    The upshot beam would fade,
And England over
    Advanced the lofty shade.

The lofty shade advances,
    I fetch my flute and play:
Come, lads, and learn the dances
    And praise the tune to-day.
To-morrow, more's the pity,
    Away we both must hie,
To air the ditty,
    And to earth I.

Thomas Hardy

Molly Gone

No more summer for Molly and me;
    There is snow on the tree,
And the blackbirds plump large as the rooks are, almost,
    And the water is hard
Where they used to dip bills at the dawn ere her figure was lost
    To these coasts, now my prison close-barred.

No more planting by Molly and me
    Where the beds used to be
Of sweet-william; no training the clambering rose
    By the framework of fir
Now bowering the pathway, whereon it swings gaily and
                               blows
    As if calling commendment from her.

No more jauntings by Molly and me
    To the town by the sea,
Or along over Whitesheet to Wynyard's green Gap,
    Catching Montacute Crest
To the right against Sedgmoor, and Corton Hill's far-distant
                               cap,
    And Pilsdon and Lewsdon to west.

No more singing by Molly to me
    In the evenings when she
Was in mood and in voice, and the candles were lit,
    And past the porch-quoin
The rays would spring out on the laurels; and dumbledores hit
    On the pane, as if wishing to join.

Where, then, is Molly, who's no more with me?
   – As I stand on this lea,
 Thinking thus, there's a many-flamed star in the air,
    That tosses a sign
That her glance is regarding its face from her home, so that
                                                          there
   Her eyes may have meetings with mine.

Rupert Brooke

Fafaïa

Stars that seem so close and bright,
Watched by lovers through the night,
Swim in emptiness, men say,
Many a mile and year away.

And yonder star that burns so white,
May have died to dust and night
Ten, maybe, or fifteen year,
Before it shines upon my dear.

Oh! often among men below,
Heart cries out to heart, I know,
And one is dust a many years,
Child, before the other hears.

Heart from heart is all as far,
Fafaïa, as star from star.

Saanapu, November, 1913

Elizabeth Jennings

A Weather Spell

Seven times seven and seven again,
Come the wind and come the rain,
Come the snow and come the heat
And come where darts of lightning meet.

Come all weather, come all ways
To join and part or walk a maze.
Come, my love, be light to start.
Let no thunder break your heart.

I will take the elements
And move their dangerous charges. Chance
Is tossed away. I give you choice
And a purpose and a voice.

I will take the dark aside,
Make the furious seas divide,
But most I'll breach the wall of you
Come the heat and come the snow.

Ted Hughes

Song

O lady, when the tipped cup of the moon blessed you
You became soft fire with a cloud's grace;
The difficult stars swam for eyes in your face;
You stood, and your shadow was my place:
You turned, your shadow turned to ice
    O my lady.

O lady, when the sea caressed you
You were a marble of foam, but dumb.
When will the stone open its tomb?
When will the waves give over their foam?
The giving comes, the taking ends.
You will not die, nor come home,
    O my lady.

O lady, when the wind kissed you
You made him music for you were a shaped shell.
I follow the waters and the wind still
Since my heart heard it and all to pieces fell
Which your lovers stole, meaning ill,
    O my lady.

O lady, consider when I shall have lost you
The moon's full hands, scattering waste,
The sea's hands, dark from the world's breast,
The world's decay where the wind's hands have passed,
And my head, worn out with love, at rest
In my hands, and my hands full of dust,
    O my lady.

W. B. Yeats

A Last Confession

What lively lad most pleasured me
Of all that with me lay?
I answer that I gave my soul
And loved in misery,
But had great pleasure with a lad
That I loved bodily.

Flinging from his arms I laughed
To think his passion such
He fancied that I gave a soul
Did but our bodies touch,
And laughed upon his breast to think
Beast gave beast as much.

I gave what other women gave
That stepped out of their clothes,
But when this soul, its body off,
Naked to naked goes,
He it has found shall find therein
What none other knows,

And give his own and take his own
And rule in his own right;
And though it loved in misery
Close and cling so tight,
There's not a bird of day that dare
Extinguish that delight.

D. H. Lawrence

To Women,
as Far as I'm Concerned

The feelings I don't have I don't have.
The feelings I don't have, I won't say I have.
The feelings you say you have, you don't have.
The feelings you would like us both to have, we neither of us
                                                      have.

The feelings people ought to have, they never have.
If people say they've got feelings, you may be pretty sure they
                                         haven't got them.

So if you want either of us to feel anything at all
you'd better abandon all idea of feelings altogether.

Ogden Nash

The People Upstairs

The people upstairs all practice ballet.
Their living room is a bowling alley.
Their bedroom is full of conducted tours.
Their radio is louder than yours.
They celebrate week ends all the week.
When they take a shower, your ceilings leak.
They try to get their parties to mix
By supplying their guests with Pogo sticks,
And when their orgy at last abates,
They go to the bathroom on roller skates.
I might love the people upstairs wondrous
If instead of above us, they just lived under us.

Thomas Hardy

'You on the Tower'

I

'You on the tower of my factory –
    What do you see up there?
Do you see Enjoyment with wide wings
    Advancing to reach me here?'
– 'Yea; I see enjoyment with wide wings
    Advancing to reach you here.'

II

'Good. Soon I'll come and ask you
    To tell me again thereon. . . .
Well, what is he doing now? Hoi, there!'
    – 'He still is flying on.'
'Ah, waiting till I have full-finished.
    Good. Tell me again anon. . . .

III

'Hoi, Watchman! I'm here. When comes he?
    Between my sweats I am chill.'
   – 'Oh, you there, working still?
Why, surely he reached you a time back,
    And took you miles from your mill?
He duly came in his winging,
    And now he has passed out of view.
How can it be that you missed him?
    He brushed you by as he flew.'

Elizabeth Jennings

Friendship

Such love I cannot analyse;
It does not rest in lips or eyes,
Neither in kisses nor caress.
Partly, I know, it's gentleness

And understanding in one word
Or in brief letters. It's preserved
By trust and by respect and awe.
These are the words I'm feeling for.

Two people, yes, two lasting friends.
The giving comes, the taking ends.
There is no measure for such things
For this all Nature slows and sings.

William Plomer

Move On

They made love under bridges, lacking beds,
And engines whistled them a bridal song,
A sudden bull's-eye showed them touching heads,
Policemen told them they were doing wrong;
And when they slept on seats in public gardens
Told them, 'Commit no nuisance in the park';
The beggars, begging the policemen's pardons,
Said that they thought as it was after dark –

At this the law grew angry and declared
Outlaws who outrage by-laws are the devil;
At this the lovers only stood and stared,
As well they might, for they had meant no evil;
'Move on,' the law said. To avoid a scene
They moved. And thus we keep our cities clean.

Charles Causley

Hawthorn White

Hawthorn white, hawthorn red
Hanging in the garden at my head
Tell me simple, tell me true
When comes the winter what must I do?

I have a house with chimneys four
I have a silver bell on the door,
A single hearth and a single bed.
   Not enough, the hawthorn said.

I have a lute, I have a lyre
I have a yellow cat by my fire,
A nightingale to my tree is tied.
   That bird looks sick, the hawthorn sighed.

I write on paper pure as milk
I lie on sheets of Shantung silk,
On my green breast no sin has snowed.
   You'll catch your death, the hawthorn crowed.

My purse is packed with a five-pound note
The watchdogs in my garden gloat.
I blow the bagpipe down my side.
   Better blow your safe, the hawthorn cried.

My pulse is steady as my clock
My wits are wise as the weathercock.
Twice a year we are overhauled.
   It's Double Summer-Time! the hawthorn called.

I have a horse with wings for feet
I have chicken each day to eat,
When I was born the church-bells rang.
   Only one at a time, the hawthorn sang.

I have a cellar, I have a spread
The bronze blood runs round my bulkhead:
Why is my heart as light as lead?
   Love is not there, the hawthorn said.

Stevie Smith

My Hat

Mother said if I wore this hat
I should be certain to get off with the right sort of chap
Well look where I am now, on a desert island
With so far as I can see no one at all on hand
I know what has happened though I suppose Mother wouldn't
    see
This hat being so strong has completely run away with me
I had the feeling it was beginning to happen the moment I put
    it on
What a moment that was as I rose up, I rose up like a flying
    swan
As strong as a swan too, why see how far my hat has flown me
    away
It took us a night to come and then a night and a day
And all the time the swan wing in my hat waved beautifully
Ah, I thought, How this hat becomes me.
First the sea was dark but then it was pale blue
And still the wing beat and we flew and we flew
A night and a day and a night, and by the old right way
Between the sun and the moon we flew until morning day.
It is always early morning here on this peculiar island
The green grass grows into the sea on the dipping land
Am I glad I am here? Yes, well, I am,
It's nice to be rid of Father, Mother and the young man
There's just one thing causes me a twinge of pain,
If I take my hat off, shall I find myself home again?
So in this early morning land I always wear my hat
Go home, you see, well I wouldn't run a risk like that.

Lady Ōtomo of Sakanoue

Sent from the Capital to her Elder Daughter

More than the gems
Locked away and treasured
In his comb-box
By the God of the Sea,
I prize you, my daughter.
But we are of this world
And such is its way!
Summoned by your man,
Obedient, you journeyed
To the far-off land of Koshi.
Since we parted,
Like a spreading vine,
Your eyebrows, pencil-arched,
Like waves about to break,
Have flitted before my eyes,
Bobbing like tiny boats.
Such is my yearning for you
That this body, time-riddled,
May well not bear the strain.

Envoy
Had I only known
My longing would be so great,
Like a clear mirror
I'd have looked on you –
Not missing a day,
Not even an hour.

Helen Waddell

Lyrics from the Chinese

V

Written in the twelfth century before Christ, c. 1121

The morning glory climbs above my head,
Pale flowers of white and purple, blue and red.
    I am disquieted.

Down in the withered grasses something stirred;
I thought it was his footfall that I heard.
    Then a grasshopper chirred.

I climbed the hill just as the new moon showed,
I saw him coming on the southern road.
    My heart lays down its load.

Sa'di Yusuf

Hamra Night

A candle in a long street
A candle in the sleep of houses
A candle for frightened shops
A candle for bakeries
A candle for a journalist trembling in an empty office
A candle for a fighter
A candle for a woman doctor watching over patients
A candle for the wounded
A candle for plain talk
A candle for the stairs
A candle for a hotel packed with refugees
A candle for a singer
A candle for broadcasters in their hideouts
A candle for a bottle of water
A candle for the air
A candle for two lovers in a naked flat
A candle for the falling sky
A candle for the beginning
A candle for the ending
A candle for the last communiqué
A candle for conscience
A candle in my hands.

Hamra: A fashionable district in Beirut

Boris Pasternak

Winter Night

Snow, snow, all the world over,
Snow to the world's end swirling,
A candle was burning on the table,
A candle burning.

As midges swarming in summer
Fly to the candle flame,
The snowflakes swarming outside
Flew at the window frame.

The blizzard etched on the window
Frosty patterning.
A candle was burning on the table,
A candle burning.

The lighted ceiling carried
A shadow frieze:
Entwining hands, entwining feet,
Entwining destinies.

And two little shoes dropped,
Thud, from the mattress.
And candle wax like tears dropped
On an empty dress.

And all was lost in a tunnel
Of grey snow churning.
A candle was burning on the table,
A candle burning.

And when a draught flattened the flame,
Temptation blazed
And like a fiery angel raised
Two cross-shaped wings.

All February the snow fell
And sometimes till morning
A candle was burning on the table,
A candle burning.

Pablo Neruda

I Like For You To Be Still

I like for you to be still: it is as though you were absent,
and you hear me from far away and my voice does not touch
you.
It seems as though your eyes had flown away
and it seems that a kiss had sealed your mouth.

As all things are filled with my soul
you emerge from the things, filled with my soul.
You appear before my soul, a daisy of dream,
with the aspect of a melancholy word.

I like for you to be still, and you seem far away.
As though you were complaining, a daisy in a lullaby.
And you hear me from far away, and my voice does not reach
you:
Let me come to be still in your silence.

And let me talk to you with your silence
that is bright as a lamp, simple as a ring.
You are like the night, with its stillness and constellations.
Your silence is that of a star, as remote and candid.

I like for you to be still: it is as though you were absent,
distant and full of sorrow as though you had died.
One word then, one smile, is enough.
And I am happy, happy at something that cannot be named.

Seamus Heaney

The Skunk

Up, black, striped and damasked like the chasuble
At a funeral mass, the skunk's tail
Paraded the skunk. Night after night
I expected her like a visitor.

The refrigerator whinnied into silence.
My desk light softened beyond the verandah.
Small oranges loomed in the orange tree.
I began to be tense as a voyeur.

After eleven years I was composing
Love-letters again, broaching the word 'wife'
Like a stored cask, as if its slender vowel
Had mutated into the night earth and air

Of California. The beautiful, useless
Tang of eucalyptus spelt your absence.
The aftermath of a mouthful of wine
Was like inhaling you off a cold pillow.

And there she was, the intent and glamorous,
Ordinary, mysterious skunk,
Mythologized, demythologized,
Snuffing the boards five feet beyond me.

It all came back to me last night, stirred
By the sootfall of your things at bedtime,
Your head-down, tail-up hunt in a bottom drawer
For the black plunge-line nightdress.

Robert Graves

To Be Called a Bear

Bears gash the forest trees
    To mark the bounds
    Of their own hunting grounds;
They follow the wild bees
    Point by point home
    For love of honeycomb;
They browse on blueberries.

Then should I stare
If I am called a bear,
And it is not the truth?
Unkempt and surly with a sweet tooth
I tilt my muzzle toward the starry hub
Where Queen Callisto guards her cub;

But envy those that here
    All winter breathing slow
    Sleep warm under the snow,
That yawn awake when the skies clear,
    And lank with longing grow
No more than one brief month a year.

John Betjeman

The Licorice Fields at Pontefract

In the licorice fields at Pontefract
    My love and I did meet
And many a burdened licorice bush
    Was blooming round our feet;
Red hair she had and golden skin,
Her sulky lips were shaped for sin,
Her sturdy legs were flannel-slack'd,
The strongest legs in Pontefract.

The light and dangling licorice flowers
    Gave off the sweetest smells;
From various black Victorian towers
    The Sunday evening bells
Came pealing over dales and hills
And tanneries and silent mills
And lowly streets where country stops
And little shuttered corner shops.

She cast her blazing eyes on me
    And plucked a licorice leaf;
I was her captive slave and she
    My red-haired robber chief.
Oh love! for love I could not speak,
It left me winded, wilting, weak
And held in brown arms strong and bare
And wound with flaming ropes of hair.

A. E. Housman

Last Poems XXI

The fairies break their dances
   And leave the printed lawn,
And up from India glances
   The silver sail of dawn.

The candles burn their sockets,
   The blinds let through the day,
The young man feels his pockets
   And wonders what's to pay.

A. E. Housman

Last Poems XXIII

In the morning, in the morning,
   In the happy field of hay,
Oh they looked at one another
   By the light of day.

In the blue and silver morning
   On the haycock as they lay,
Oh they looked at one another
   And they looked away.

Rupert Brooke

The Hill

Breathless, we flung us on the windy hill,
    Laughed in the sun, and kissed the lovely grass.
    You said, 'Through glory and ecstasy we pass;
Wind, sun, and earth remain, and the birds sing still,
When we are old, are old. . . .' 'And when we die
    All's over that is ours; and life burns on
Through other lovers, other lips,' said I,
    'Heart of my heart, our heaven is now, is won!'

'We are Earth's best, that learnt her lesson here.
    Life is our cry. We have kept the faith!' we said;
    'We shall go down with unreluctant tread
Rose-crowned into the darkness!' . . . Proud we were,
And laughed, that had such brave true things to say.
– And then you suddenly cried, and turned away.

Elizabeth Jennings

Love Poem

There is a shyness that we have
Only with those whom we most love.
Something it has to do also
With how we cannot bring to mind
A face whose every line we know.
O love is kind, O love is kind.

That there should still remain the first
Sweetness, also the later thirst –
This is why pain must play some part
In all true feelings that we find
And every shaking of the heart.
O love is kind, O love is kind.

And it is right that we should want
Discretion, secrecy, no hint
Of what we share. Love which cries out,
And wants the world to understand,
Is love that holds itself in doubt.
For love is quiet, and love is kind.

Edwin Muir

For
Ann Scott-Moncrieff
(1914–1943)

Dear Ann, wherever you are
Since you lately learnt to die,
You are this unsetting star
That shines unchanged in my eye;
So near, inaccessible,
Absent and present so much
Since out of the world you fell,
Fell from hearing and touch –
So near. But your mortal tongue
Used for immortal use,
The grace of a woman young,
The air of an early muse,
The wealth of the chambered brow
And soaring flight of your eyes:
These are no longer now.
Death has a princely prize.

You who were Ann much more
Than others are that or this,
Extravagant over the score
To be what only is,
Would you not still say now
What you once used to say
Of the great Why and How,
On that or the other day?

For though of your heritage
The minority here began,
Now you have come of age
And are entirely Ann.

Under the years' assaults,
In the storm of good and bad,
You too had the faults
That Emily Brontë had,
Ills of body and soul,
Of sinner and saint and all
Who strive to make themselves whole,
Smashed to bits by the Fall.
Yet 'the world is a pleasant place'
I can hear your voice repeat,
While the sun shone in your face
Last summer in Princes Street.

Edwin Muir

In Love for Long

I've been in love for long
With what I cannot tell
And will contrive a song
For the intangible
That has no mould or shape,
From which there's no escape.

It is not even a name,
Yet is all constancy;
Tried or untried, the same,
It cannot part from me;
A breath, yet as still
As the established hill.

It is not any thing,
And yet all being is;
Being, being, being,
Its burden and its bliss.
How can I ever prove
What it is I love?

This happy happy love
Is sieged with crying sorrows,
Crushed beneath and above
Between to-days and morrows;
A little paradise
Held in the world's vice.

And there it is content
And careless as a child,
And in imprisonment
Flourishes sweet and wild;
In wrong, beyond wrong,
All the world's day long.

This love a moment known
For what I do not know
And in a moment gone
Is like the happy doe
That keeps its perfect laws
Between the tiger's paws
And vindicates its cause.

Walter de la Mare

All That's Past

Very old are the woods;
    And the buds that break
Out of the brier's boughs,
    When March winds wake,
So old with their beauty are –
    Oh, no man knows
Through what wild centuries
    Roves back the rose.

Very old are the brooks;
    And the rills that rise
Where snow sleeps cold beneath
    The azure skies
Sing such a history
    Of come and gone,
Their every drop is as wise
    As Solomon.

Very old are we men;
    Our dreams are tales
Told in dim Eden
    By Eve's nightingales;
We wake and whisper awhile,
    But, the day gone by,
Silence and sleep like fields
    Of amaranth lie.

John Crowe Ransom

Here Lies a Lady

Here lies a lady of beauty and high degree.
Of chills and fever she died, of fever and chills,
The delight of her husband, her aunt, an infant of three,
And of medicos marveling sweetly on her ills.

For either she burned, and her confident eyes would blaze,
And her fingers fly in a manner to puzzle their heads –
What was she making? Why, nothing; she sat in a maze
Of old scraps of laces, snipped into curious shreds –

Or this would pass, and the light of her fire decline
Till she lay discouraged and cold, like a stalk white and
blown,
And would not open her eyes, to kisses, to wine;
The sixth of these states was her last; the cold settled down.

Sweet ladies, long may ye bloom, and toughly I hope ye may
thole,
But was she not lucky? In flowers and lace and mourning,
In love and great honour we bade God rest her soul
After six little spaces of chill, and six of burning.

Helen Waddell

9th Century Requiem

Lament for Hathimoda,
Abbess of Gandesheim

Thou hast come safe to port
   I still at sea.
The light is on thy head
   Darkness in me.
Pluck thou in heaven's fields
   Violet and rose
While I strew flowers
   That will thy vigil keep,
Where thou dost sleep, love,
   In thy last repose.

Laurie Lee

Boy in Ice

O river, green and still,
By frost and memory stayed,
Your dumb and stiffened glass divides
A shadow and a shade.

In air, the shadow's face
My winter gaze lets fall
To see beneath the stream's bright bars
That other shade in thrall.

A boy, time-fixed in ice,
His cheeks with summer dyed,
His mouth, a rose-devouring rose,
His bird-throat petrified.

O fabulous and lost,
More distant to me now
Than rock-drawn mammoth, painted stag
Or tigers in the snow.

You stare into my face
Dead as ten thousand years,
Your sparrow tongue sealed in my mouth
Your world about my ears.

And till our shadows meet,
Till time burns through the ice,
Thus frozen shall we ever stay
Locked in this paradise.

Walter de la Mare

Alexander

It was the Great Alexander,
    Capped with a golden helm,
Sate in the ages, in his floating ship,
    In a dead calm.

Voices of sea-maids singing
    Wandered across the deep:
The sailors labouring on their oars
    Rowed, as in sleep.

All the high pomp of Asia,
    Charmed by that siren lay,
Out of their weary and dreaming minds,
    Faded away.

Like a bold boy sate their Captain
    His glamour withered and gone,
In the souls of his brooding mariners,
    While the song pined on.

Time, like a falling dew,
    Life, like the scene of a dream,
Laid between slumber and slumber,
    Only did seem. . . .

O Alexander, then,
    In all us mortals too,
Wax thou not bold – too bold
    On the wave dark-blue!

Come the calm, infinite night,
　　Who then will hear
Aught save the singing
　　Of the sea-maids clear?

Rudyard Kipling

Cities and Thrones and Powers
(*from* Puck of Pook's Hill)

Cities and Thrones and Powers
   Stand in Time's eye,
Almost as long as flowers,
   Which daily die:
But, as new buds put forth
   To glad new men,
Out of the spent and unconsidered Earth
   The Cities rise again.

This season's Daffodil,
   She never hears
What change, what chance, what chill,
   Cut down last year's:
But with bold countenance,
   And knowledge small,
Esteems her seven days' continuance
   To be perpetual.

So Time that is o'er-kind
   To all that be,
Ordains us e'en as blind,
   As bold as she:
That in our very death,
   And burial sure,
Shadow to shadow, well persuaded, saith
   'See how our works endure!'

John Betjeman

Mortality

The first-class brains of a senior civil servant
    Shiver and shatter and fall
As the steering column of his comfortable Humber
    Batters in the bony wall.
All those delicate little re-adjustments
    'On the one hand, if we proceed
With the *ad hoc* policy hitherto adapted
    To individual need . . .
On the other hand, too rigid an arrangement
    Might, of itself, perforce . . .
I would like to submit for the Minister's concurrence
    The following alternative course,
Subject to revision and reconsideration
    In the light our experience gains . . .'
And this had to happen at the corner where the by-pass
    Comes into Egham out of Staines.
That very near miss for an All Souls' Fellowship
    The recent compensation of a 'K' –
The first-class brains of a senior civil servant
    Are sweetbread on the road today.

William Plomer

Miss Robinson's Funeral

A cold afternoon, and death looks prouder
As mourning motors mourning motors follow,
One solemn as another. Lilies shiver,
Carnations also shiver, while the hollow
Seagulls search for offal in the river
And a woman burrows in her bag for powder.

The undertakers don't observe the scenery
And nothing moves them but the wheels they glide on,
The undertakers undertake to bury
(How black the motor cars they ride on),
They are not volatile or sad or merry,
Neither are waxworks going by machinery.

The coffin's full, and the time is after four;
The grave is empty, earth joins earth once more –
But the ghost of the late Miss Robinson is floating
Backside upwards in the air with a smile across her jaw:
She was tickled to death, and is carefully noting
Phenomena she never thought of noticing before.

e. e. cummings

my sweet old etcetera

my sweet old etcetera
aunt lucy during the recent

war could and what
is more did tell you just
what everybody was fighting

for,
my sister

isabel created hundreds
(and
hundreds) of socks not to
mention shirts fleaproof earwarmers

etcetera wristers etcetera, my
mother hoped that

i would die etcetera
bravely of course my father used
to become hoarse talking about how it was
a privilege and if only he
could meanwhile my

self etcetera lay quietly
in the deep mud et

cetera
(dreaming,
et
   cetera, of
Your smile
eyes knees and of your Etcetera)

T. S. Eliot

Grizabella: the Glamour Cat

She haunted many a low resort
Near the grimy road of Tottenham Court;
She flitted about the No Man's Land
From The Rising Sun to The Friend at Hand.
And the postman sighed, as he scratched his head:
'You'd really ha' thought she'd ought to be dead
And who would ever suppose that *that*
was Grizabella, the Glamour Cat!'

(Grizabella was an unpublished fragment,
till she made her appearance in the libretto of *Cats*.
'Memory' is her song.)

Trevor Nunn

Memory

Midnight, not a sound from the pavement.
Has the moon lost her memory?
She is smiling alone.
In the lamp light the withered leaves collect at my feet
And the wind begins to moan.

Memory. All alone in the moonlight
I can smile at the old days.
I was beautiful then.
I remember the time I knew what happiness was,
Let the memory live again.

Every street lamp seems to beat a fatalistic warning
Someone mutters and the street lamp gutters,
And soon it will be morning.

Daylight. I must wait for the sunrise
I must think of a new life
And I mustn't give in.
When the dawn comes the night will be a memory, too
And a new day will begin.

Burnt-out ends of smoky days
The stale cold smell of morning.
The street-lamp dies, another night is over,
Another day is dawning.

Touch me. It's so easy to leave me
All alone with the memory
Of my days in the sun.
If you touch me you'll understand what happiness is.
Look, a new day has begun.

A. E. Housman

In Valleys Green and Still

In valleys green and still
    Where lovers wander maying
They hear from over hill
    A music playing.

Behind the drum and fife,
    Past hawthornwood and hollow,
Through earth and out of life
    The soldiers follow.

The soldier's is the trade:
    In any wind or weather
He steals the heart of maid
    And man together.

The lover and his lass
    Beneath the hawthorn lying
Have heard the soldiers pass,
    And both are sighing.

And down the distance they
    With dying note and swelling
Walk the resounding way
    To the still dwelling.

Wilfred Owen

Miners

There was a whispering in my hearth,
    A sigh of the coal,
Grown wistful of a former earth
    It might recall.

I listened for a tale of leaves
    And smothered ferns;
Frond-forests; and the low, sly lives
    Before the fawns.

My fire might show steam-phantoms simmer
    From Time's old cauldron,
Before the birds made nests in summer,
    Or men had children.

But the coals were murmuring of their mine,
    And moans down there
Of boys that slept wry sleep, and men
    Writhing for air.

And I saw white bones in the cinder-shard.
    Bones without number;
For many hearts with coal are charred
    And few remember.

I thought of some who worked dark pits
    Of war, and died
Digging the rock where Death reputes
    Peace lies indeed.

Comforted years will sit soft-chaired
    In rooms of amber;
The years will stretch their hands, well-cheered
    By our lives' ember.

The centuries will burn rich loads
    With which we groaned,
Whose warmth shall lull their dreaming lids
    While songs are crooned.
But they will not dream of us poor lads
    Lost in the ground.

Léopold Sédar Senghor

Be Not Amazed

Be not amazed beloved, if sometimes my song grows dark,
If I exchange the lyrical reed for the Khalam or the tama
And the green scent of the ricefields, for the swiftly galloping
                                      war drums.
I hear the threats of ancient deities, the furious cannonade of
                                      the god.
Oh, tomorrow perhaps, the purple voice of your bard will be
                                      silent for ever.
That is why my rhythm becomes so fast, that the fingers bleed
                                      on the Khalam.
Perhaps, beloved, I shall fall tomorrow, on a restless earth
Lamenting your sinking eyes, and the dark tom-tom of the
                                      mortars below.
And you will weep in the twilight for the glowing voice that
                                      sang your black beauty.

Siegfried Sassoon

In the Pink

So Davies wrote: 'This leaves me in the pink'.
Then scrawled his name: 'Your loving sweetheart, Willie'.
With crosses for a hug. He'd had a drink
Of rum and tea; and, though the barn was chilly,
For once his blood ran warm; he had pay to spend.
Winter was passing; soon the year would mend.

But he couldn't sleep that night; stiff in the dark
He groaned and thought of Sundays at the farm,
And how he'd go as cheerful as a lark
In his best suit, to wander arm in arm
With brown-eyed Gwen, and whisper in her ear
The simple, silly things she liked to hear.

And then he thought: to-morrow night we trudge
Up to the trenches, and my boots are rotten.
Five miles of stodgy clay and freezing sludge,
And everything but wretchedness forgotten.
To-night he's in the pink; but soon he'll die.
And still the war goes on – *he* don't know why.

Siegfried Sassoon

At the Cenotaph

I saw the Prince of Darkness, with his Staff,
Standing bare-headed by the Cenotaph:
Unostentatious and respectful, there
He stood, and offered up the following prayer.
    'Make them forget, O Lord, what this Memorial
      Means; their discredited ideas revive;
    Breed new belief that War is purgatorial
      Proof of the pride and power of being alive;
    Men's biologic urge to readjust
      The Map of Europe, Lord of Hosts, increase;
    Lift up their hearts in large destructive lust;
      And crown their heads with blind vindictive
                              Peace.'
The Prince of Darkness to the Cenotaph
Bowed. As he walked away I heard him laugh.

Robert Frost

Fire and Ice

Some say the world will end in fire,
Some say in ice.
From what I've tasted of desire
I hold with those who favor fire.
But if it had to perish twice,
I think I know enough of hate
To say that for destruction ice
Is also great
And would suffice.

C. P. Cavafy

The Horses of Achilles

When they saw Patroklos dead
– so brave and strong, so young –
the horses of Achilles began to weep;
their immortal natures were outraged
by this work of death they had to look at.
They reared their heads, tossed their manes,
beat the ground with their hooves,
and mourned Patroklos, seeing him lifeless, destroyed,
now mere flesh only, his spirit gone,
defenceless, without breath,
turned back from life to the great Nothingness.

Zeus saw the tears of those immortal horses and felt sorry.
'I shouldn't have acted so thoughtlessly
at the wedding of Peleus,' he said.
'Better if we hadn't given you as a gift,
my unhappy horses. What business did you have down
                                              there,
among pathetic human beings, the toys of fate?
You're free of death, you won't get old,
yet ephemeral disasters torment you.
Men have caught you in their misery.'
But it was for the eternal disaster of death
that those two gallant horses shed their tears.

Stevie Smith

My Heart Goes Out

My heart goes out to my Creator in love
Who gave me Death, as end and remedy.
All living creatures come to quiet Death
For him to eat up their activity
And give them nothing, which is what they want although
When they are living they do not think so.

Elizabeth Jennings

One Flesh

Lying apart now, each in a separate bed,
He with a book, keeping the light on late,
She like a girl dreaming of childhood,
All men elsewhere – it is as if they wait
Some new event: the book he holds unread,
Her eyes fixed on the shadows overhead.

Tossed up like flotsam from a former passion,
How cool they lie. They hardly ever touch,
Or if they do it is like a confession
Of having little feeling – or too much.
Chastity faces them, a destination
For which their whole lives were a preparation.

Strangely apart, yet strangely close together,
Silence between them like a thread to hold
And not wind in. And time itself's a feather
Touching them gently. Do they know they're old,
These two who are my father and my mother
Whose fire from which I came, has now grown cold?

W. B. Yeats

Girl's Song

I went out alone
To sing a song or two,
My fancy on a man,
And you know who.

Another came in sight
That on a stick relied
To hold himself upright:
I sat and cried.

And that was all my song –
When everything is told,
Saw I an old man young
Or young man old?

C. P. Cavafy

An Old Man

At the noisy end of the café, head bent
over the table, an old man sits alone,
a newspaper in front of him.

And in the miserable banality of old age
he thinks how little he enjoyed the years
when he had strength, and wit, and looks.

He knows he's very old now: sees it, feels it.
Yet it seems he was young just yesterday.
The time's gone by so quickly, gone by so quickly.

And he thinks how Discretion fooled him,
how he always believed, so stupidly,
that cheat who said: 'Tomorrow. You have plenty of time.'

He remembers impulses bridled, the joy
he sacrificed. Every chance he lost
now mocks his brainless prudence.

But so much thinking, so much remembering
makes the old man dizzy. He falls asleep,
his head resting on the café table.

Rabindranath Tagore

Grandfather's Holiday

Blue sky, paddy fields, grandchild's play,
Deep ponds, diving-stage, child's holiday;
Tree shade, barn corners, catch-me-if-you-dare,
Undergrowth, *pārul*-bushes, life without care.
Green paddy all a-quiver, hopeful as a child,
Child prancing, river dancing, waves running wild.

Bespectacled grandfather old man am I,
Trapped in my work like a spiderwebbed fly.
Your games are my games, my proxy holiday,
Your laugh the sweetest music I shall ever play.
Your joy is mine, my mischief in your eyes,
Your delight the country where my freedom lies.

Autumn sailing in, now, steered by your play,
Bringing white *śiuli*-flowers to grace your holiday.
Pleasure of the chilly air tingling me at night,
Blown from Himālaya on the breeze of your delight.
Dawn in Āśvin, flower-forcing roseate sun,
Dressed in the colours of a grandchild's fun.

Flooding of my study with your leaps and your capers,
Work gone, books flying, avalanche of papers.
Arms round my neck, in my lap bounce thump –
Hurricane of freedom in my heart as you jump.
Who has taught you, how he does it, I shall never know –
You're the one who teaches me to let myself go.

W. B. Yeats

The Song of Wandering Aengus

I went out to the hazel wood,
Because a fire was in my head,
And cut and peeled a hazel wand,
And hooked a berry to a thread;
And when white moths were on the wing,
And moth-like stars were flickering out,
I dropped the berry in a stream
And caught a little silver trout.

When I had laid it on the floor
I went to blow the fire aflame,
But something rustled on the floor,
And some one called me by my name:
It had become a glimmering girl
With apple blossom in her hair
Who called me by my name and ran
And faded through the brightening air.

Though I am old with wandering
Through hollow lands and hilly lands,
I will find out where she has gone,
And kiss her lips and take her hands;
And walk among long dappled grass,
And pluck till time and times are done
The silver apples of the moon,
The golden apples of the sun.

W. H. Auden

If I Could Tell You

Time will say nothing but I told you so,
Time only knows the price we have to pay;
If I could tell you I would let you know.

If we should weep when clowns put on their show,
If we should stumble when musicians play,
Time will say nothing but I told you so.

There are no fortunes to be told, although,
Because I love you more than I can say,
If I could tell you I would let you know.

The winds must come from somewhere when they blow,
There must be reasons why the leaves decay;
Time will say nothing but I told you so.

Perhaps the roses really want to grow,
The vision seriously intends to stay;
If I could tell you I would let you know.

Suppose the lions all get up and go,
And all the brooks and soldiers run away;
Will Time say nothing but I told you so?
If I could tell you I would let you know.

October, 1940

Stevie Smith

The Airy Christ
After reading Dr Rieu's translation of St Mark's Gospel

Who is this that comes in splendour, coming from the blazing East?
This is he we had not thought of, this is he the airy Christ.

Airy, in an airy manner in an airy parkland walking,
Others take him by the hand, lead him, do the talking.

But the Form, the airy One, frowns an airy frown,
What they say he knows must be, but he looks aloofly down,

Looks aloofly at his feet, looks aloofly at his hands,
Knows they must, as prophets say, nailèd be to wooden bands.

As he knows the words he sings, that he sings so happily
Must be changed to working laws, yet sings he ceaselessly.

Those who truly hear the voice, the words, the happy song,
Never shall need working laws to keep from doing wrong.

Deaf men will pretend sometimes they hear the song, the words,
And make excuse to sin extremely; this will be absurd.

Heed it not. Whatever foolish men may do the song is cried
For those who hear, and the sweet singer does not care that he was crucified.

For he does not wish that men should love him more than anything
Because he died; he only wishes they would hear him sing.

Dylan Thomas

The Conversation of Prayer

The conversation of prayers about to be said
By the child going to bed and the man on the stairs
Who climbs to his dying love in her high room,
The one not caring to whom in his sleep he will move
And the other full of tears that she will be dead,

Turns in the dark on the sound they know will arise
Into the answering skies from the green ground,
From the man on the stairs and the child by his bed,
The sound about to be said in the two prayers
For the sleep in a safe land and the love who dies

Will be the same grief flying. Whom shall they calm?
Shall the child sleep unharmed or the man be crying?
The conversation of prayers about to be said
Turns on the quick and the dead, and the man on the stairs
To-night shall find no dying but alive and warm

In the fire of his care his love in the high room.
And the child not caring to whom he climbs his prayer
Shall drown in a grief as deep as his true grave,
And mark the dark eyed wave, through the eyes of sleep,
Dragging him up the stairs to one who lies dead.

Sylvia Plath

The Arrival of the Bee Box

I ordered this, this clean wood box
Square as a chair and almost too heavy to lift.
I would say it was the coffin of a midget
Or a square baby
Were there not such a din in it.

The box is locked, it is dangerous.
I have to live with it overnight
And I can't keep away from it.
There are no windows, so I can't see what is in there.
There is only a little grid, no exit.

I put my eye to the grid.
It is dark, dark,
With the swarmy feeling of African hands
Minute and shrunk for export,
Black on black, angrily clambering.

How can I let them out?
It is the noise that appals me most of all,
The unintelligible syllables.
It is like a Roman mob,
Small, taken one by one, but my god, together!

I lay my ear to furious Latin.
I am not a Caesar.
I have simply ordered a box of maniacs.
They can be sent back.
They can die, I need feed them nothing, I am the owner.

I wonder how hungry they are.
I wonder if they would forget me
If I just undid the locks and stood back and turned into a tree.
There is the laburnum, its blond colonnades,
And the petticoats of the cherry.

They might ignore me immediately
In my moon suit and funeral veil.
I am no source of honey
So why should they turn on me?
Tomorrow I will be sweet God, I will set them free.

The box is only temporary.

Charles Causley

I Am the Great Sun
(From a Normandy crucifix of 1632)

I am the great sun, but you do not see me,
  I am your husband, but you turn away.
I am the captive, but you do not free me,
  I am the captain you will not obey.

I am the truth, but you will not believe me,
  I am the city where you will not stay,
I am your wife, your child, but you will leave me,
  I am that God to whom you will not pray.

I am your counsel, but you do not hear me,
  I am the lover whom you will betray,
I am the victor, but you do not cheer me,
  I am the holy dove whom you will slay.

I am your life, but if you will not name me,
Seal up your soul with tears, and never blame me.

Acknowledgements

The editor and publishers gratefully acknowledge permission to reproduce copyright poems in this book:

'If I Could Tell You' by W. H. Auden taken from *Collected Poems* by permission of Faber & Faber Ltd. 'Licorice Fields at Pontefract' and 'Mortality' by John Betjeman taken from *Collected Poems* by permission of John Murray Publishers Ltd. 'Hawthorn White' and 'I am the Great Sun' by Charles Causley, taken from *Collected Poems* by permission of David Higham Associates on behalf of the trustees for the copyrights for Charles Causley and Macmillan London Ltd. 'An Old Man' and 'The Horses of Achilles' by C. P. Cavafy taken from *Collected Poems*, translated by Edmund Keeley and Philip Sherrard, by permission of The Hogarth Press on behalf of the Estate of Cavafy. 'my sweet old etcetera' by e. e. cummings, taken from *Collected Poems 1913–1962* by permission of Grafton Books, a division of The Collins Publishing Group. 'Alexander' and 'All That's Past' by Walter de la Mare taken from *Collected Poems* and reprinted by permission of the Society of Authors on behalf of the trustees for the copyright for Walter de la Mare. 'Grizabella the Glamour Cat' by T. S. Eliot, taken from *Cats: The Book of the Musical* by permission of Faber & Faber Ltd. 'Fire and Ice' by Robert Frost, taken from *The Poetry of Robert Frost*, edited by Edward Connery Lathem, by permission of Jonathan Cape Ltd on behalf of the Estate of Robert Frost. 'Allie', 'Song: Dew-Drop and Diamond' and 'To Be Called a Bear' by Robert Graves taken from *Collected Poems* (1975) by permission of A. P. Watt Ltd on behalf of the Executors of the Estate of Robert Graves. 'The Skunk' by Seamus Heaney taken from *Fieldwork* by permission of Faber & Faber Ltd. 'Song' by Ted Hughes taken from *The Hawk in the Rain*, reprinted by permission of Faber & Faber Ltd. 'A Weather Spell', 'Friendship', 'Love Poem' and 'One Flesh' by Elizabeth Jennings taken from *Selected Poems* by permission of David Higham Associates on behalf of the trustees for the copyrights of Elizabeth Jennings and Carcanet Press. 'Cities and Thrones and Powers' by Rudyard Kipling reprinted by permission of Hodder & Stoughton Ltd. 'To Women, as Far as I'm Concerned' by D. H. Lawrence, taken from *Complete Poems* edited by Vivian de Sola and F. Warren Roben, to the Estate of Mrs Frieda Lawrence Ravagli and Lawrence Pollinger Ltd. 'Boy in Ice' by Laurie Lee, taken from *Selected Poems* by permission of A. D. Peters. 'For Ann Scott-Moncrieff' and 'In Love For Long' by Edwin Muir, taken from *Collected Poems*, by permission of Faber & Faber Ltd. 'The People Upstairs' by Ogden Nash, taken from *Custard and Company* selected by Quentin Blake, by permission of Penguin Books Ltd. 'I Like For You To Be Still' by Pablo Neruda, taken from *Twenty Love Poems and A Song of Despair*, translated by W. S Merwin by permission of Jonathan Cape Ltd, on behalf of the Estate of Pablo Neruda. 'Memory' by Trevor Nunn, incorporating lines from Eliot's *Rhapsody on a Windy Night and other Prufrock Poems*, from *Cats: The Book of the Musical* based on *Old Possum's Book of Practical Cats* by T. S. Eliot, by permission of Faber & Faber Ltd. 'Sent from the Capital to her Elder Daughter' by Lady Ōtomo of Sakanoue, taken from *The Penguin Book of Japanese Verse*, translated by Geoffrey Bowman and Anthony Thwaite, by permission of Penguin Books Ltd. 'Miners' by Wilfred Owen taken from *The Penguin Book of Georgian Poetry* selected by James Reeves. 'Winter Night' by Boris Pasternak, taken from *Selected Poems*, translated by Jon Stallworthy and Peter France (Penguin Modern European Poets 1983), copyright Peter France. 'Arrival of the Bee Box' and 'Morning Song' by Sylvia Plath reprinted by permission of Olwyn Hughes. 'Miss Robinson's Funeral' and 'Move On' by William Plomer taken from *Collected Poems* by permission of A. P. Watt Ltd on behalf of the Estate of William Plomer. 'Here Lies a Lady' by John Crowe Ransom, from *Selected Poems*, copyright 1924 by Alfred A. Knopf, Inc. and renewed 1952 by John Crowe Ransom, by permission of the proprietors, Alfred A. Knopf, Inc. and the publishers, Eyre Methuen Ltd. 'Adam', 'Eve' and 'The Merry-go-round' by Rainer Maria Rilke, from *Selected Works* published by The Hogarth Press 1960, copyright the Estate of J. B. Leishmann. 'At the Cenotaph', 'In the Pink' and 'IV' (From: 'The Heart's Journey' by Siegfried Sassoon, taken from *Collected Poems of Siegfried Sassoon 1908–1956* by permission of George Sassoon on behalf of the Estate of Siegfried Sassoon. 'Be Not Amazed' by Léopold Sédar Senghor, taken from *The Penguin Book of Modern African Poetry*, copyright Editions du Seuil 1961, Paris. 'The Airy Christ', 'A Dream of Nourishment', 'My Hat' and 'My Heart Goes Out', by Stevie Smith, taken from *Collected Poems of Stevie Smith* (Penguin Modern Classics) by permission of the Executor, James MacGibbon. 'Grandfather's Holiday' by Rabindranath Tagore, from *Selected Poems*, translated by William Radice (Penguin Modern Classics 1985) copyright William Radice 1985, by permission of Penguin Books. 'A Conversation of Prayer' and 'Fern Hill' by Dylan Thomas, taken from *Collected Poems 1934–1952*, by permission of David Higham Associates on behalf of the trustees for the copyrights of Dylan Thomas and J. M. Dent. *Lyrics from the Chinese*: v, by Helen Waddell, by permission of Constable Publishers. 'Girl's Song', 'Song of the Wandering Aengus' and 'A Last Confession' by W. B. Yeats from *Collected Poems*, by permission of A. P. Watt Ltd on behalf of Michael B. Yeats and Macmillan London Ltd. 'Hamra Night' by Sa'di Yusuf, taken from *Modern Poetry of the Arab World*, translated by Abdullah al-Udhari, copyright Abdullah al-Udhari, 1986.

Every effort has been made to trace copyright holders, but in a few cases this has proved impossible. The editor and publishers apologize for these cases of unwilling copyright transgression and would like to hear from any copyright holders not acknowledged.

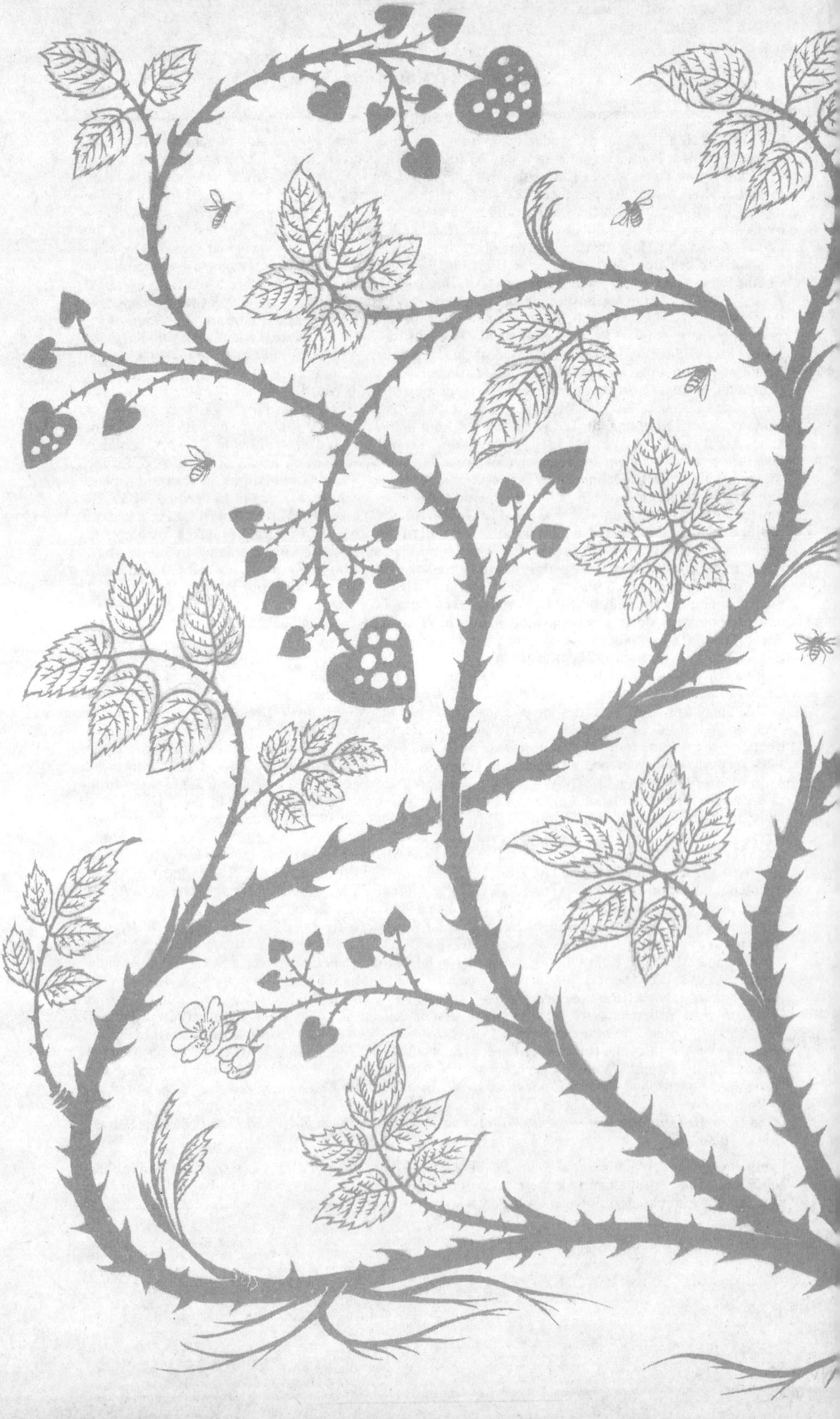